Nuclear Meltdowns

Kirsten W. Larson

Educational Media

rourkeeducationalmedia.com

Scan for Related Titles
and Teacher Resources

Before Reading:

Building Academic Vocabulary and Background Knowledge

Before reading a book, it is important to tap into what your child or students already know about the topic. This will help them develop their vocabulary, increase their reading comprehension, and make connections across the curriculum.

1. Look at the cover of the book. What will this book be about?
2. What do you already know about the topic?
3. Let's study the Table of Contents. What will you learn about in the book's chapters?
4. What would you like to learn about this topic? Do you think you might learn about it from this book? Why or why not?
5. Use a reading journal to write about your knowledge of this topic. Record what you already know about the topic and what you hope to learn about the topic.
6. Read the book.
7. In your reading journal, record what you learned about the topic and your response to the book.
8. After reading the book complete the activities below.

Content Area Vocabulary
Read the list. What do these words mean?

atoms
cores
electrons
evacuate
generators
meltdown
neutrons
nuclear energy
nucleus
protons
radiation
radioactive
tsunami
turbine
uranium

After Reading:

Comprehension and Extension Activity

After reading the book, work on the following questions with your child or students in order to check their level of reading comprehension and content mastery.

1. What is the purpose of the cooling tower? (Summarize)
2. Why is nuclear power a hot-button issue? (Infer)
3. What are some ways to prepare your community for a nuclear meltdown? (Text to self connection)
4. What percentage of electricity in the US is produced by nuclear power plants? (Summarize)
5. Where do you think power plants should be built? (Asking questions)

Extension Activity

Nuclear fission is a chain reaction, which is like a domino effect of colliding atoms. To demonstrate the chain reaction of nuclear fission, gather dominoes and a wood block or similar object. Set up a track of dominoes by standing them up and placing them close together so that each will hit the next. Tip the first domino into the second. What happened? How is this like nuclear fission? What would happen if you had an endless supply of dominoes? Now set up the track of dominoes again but place the block in between two dominoes. Tip the first domino into the second. What was different? Raise the block so that the resting domino falls into the next. What does that block represent? Why is it important to have a control rod in a nuclear reactor?

Table of Contents

Mammoth Meltdown!

On March 11, 2011, Japanese nuclear worker Takashi Sato wrote reports on his computer. It was just another day at the Fukushima Daiichi nuclear power plant about 160 miles (267 kilometers) northeast of Tokyo. The skies were clear. The sun shone. But at 2:46 p.m. everything changed.

An enormous earthquake rattled Japan. Centered 80 miles (129 kilometers) offshore in the Pacific, the Tohoku Earthquake measured 9.0 on the Richter Scale. It shook buildings for a full five minutes, sending workers ducking for cover.

That colossal quake was just the beginning. Forty-five minutes later, a wall of water struck the shore, engulfing the nuclear plant. It was a **tsunami**. American Carl Pillitteri, who also worked at the plant, said the wave was so massive it swept away the walls of the plant. What Takashi and Carl did not know was that the earthquake and tsunami would kick off one of the worst nuclear disasters in history: a **meltdown**.

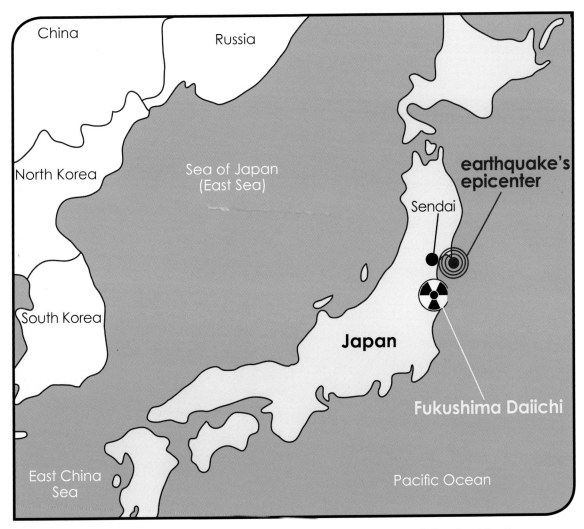

Japan sits in an area known as the Ring of Fire. This part of the Pacific Ocean experiences frequent volcanic eruptions, earthquakes, and tsunamis. The Tohoku Earthquake was one of many devastating earthquakes that have affected the country.

After the initial earthquake, workers rushing from buildings saw pipes bursting. Some pipes carried water to cool three nuclear reactors. The power went out, plunging the entire plant into darkness. Without power, pumps couldn't circulate cool water through the reactor. When temperatures climb high enough, the fuel rods melt. This is a nuclear meltdown. During a meltdown, the fuel may melt through the floor and dump **radioactive** material into the ground or water or release it into the air. Even after the nuclear reactions stop automatically, as they did at Fukushima Daiichi, nuclear **cores** stay hot.

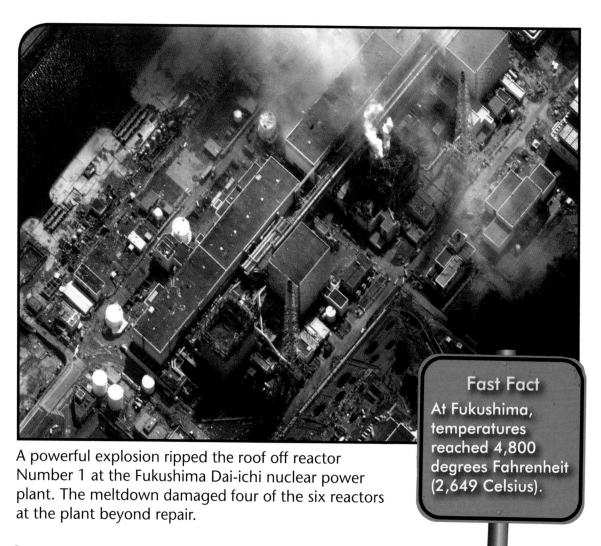

A powerful explosion ripped the roof off reactor Number 1 at the Fukushima Dai-ichi nuclear power plant. The meltdown damaged four of the six reactors at the plant beyond repair.

Fast Fact

At Fukushima, temperatures reached 4,800 degrees Fahrenheit (2,649 Celsius).

Fortunately, the power plant's backup power system came on after the earthquake. Diesel-fuel-powered **generators** switched on to make electricity and keep the cooling pumps operating. Unfortunately, those backup generators were located in the plant's basement. When the tsunami waves struck, they ruined the generators.

Diesel generators use diesel fuel—a form of gasoline—to create electricity. Aside from these bus-sized generators, nuclear power plants in the United States also have portable steam generators.

The earthquake and tsunami killed almost 16,000 people and injured another 5,000. The nuclear meltdown of three reactors at the plant lasted for more than a week. During that time, the Japanese government ordered people living within 12 miles (19 kilometers) of the plant to leave their homes as explosions at the plant spewed radioactive material into the sky. More than 80,000 people left, not returning home for months. Some still have not been able to return.

The nuclear meltdown was not the only disaster Japan faced after the massive earthquake. The tsunami washed away many towns and ports in a 216 square mile (560 square kilometer) area. It destroyed more than a million buildings.

The former Soviet Union built nuclear-powered submarines like this one in the 1970s. Today, the United States Navy has 74 nuclear-powered submarines.

Today, **nuclear energy** is all around us. In the United States, nuclear power plants generate 20 percent of the country's electricity. Nuclear power also is used to diagnose and treat cancer and power submarines and spacecraft. How do we make sure nuclear power stays safe? And how can we protect ourselves when meltdowns happen?

Nuclear Energy Nuts and Bolts

Nuclear energy starts with **atoms**, the smallest building blocks of matter. Negatively charged particles called **electrons** orbit the atom's **nucleus** like planets orbiting the Sun. The nucleus contains positively charged **protons** and **neutrons**, which have no charge. The two types of particles are held together by a strong nuclear force. In 1938, scientists tried to overcome this strong nuclear force by shooting neutrons at the element **uranium**. The neutrons split apart the nuclei, releasing energy in the process.

Fission

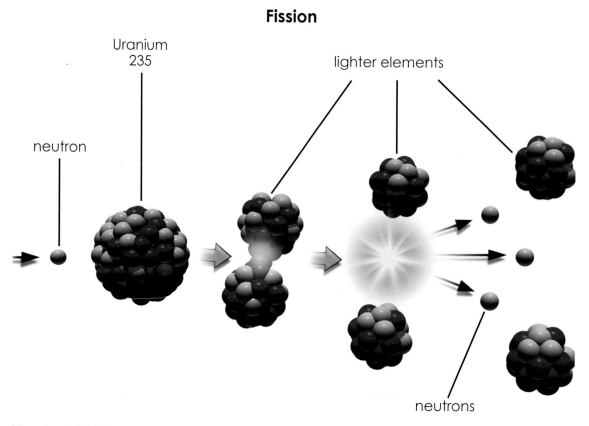

Uranium 235

lighter elements

neutron

neutrons

Uranium 235 is a common nuclear fuel. It is a special type of uranium that is relatively scarce. Special facilities separate Uranium 235 from other forms, so it can be used in nuclear reactions.

The process of bombarding atoms with neutrons to break them apart is called nuclear fission. Nuclear reactors use fission to create tremendous amounts of power. During a fission chain reaction, neutrons break up nuclei, releasing energy and more neutrons. Those newly released neutrons go on to split up more nuclei. Once started, a chain reaction is like a series of dominoes falling down.

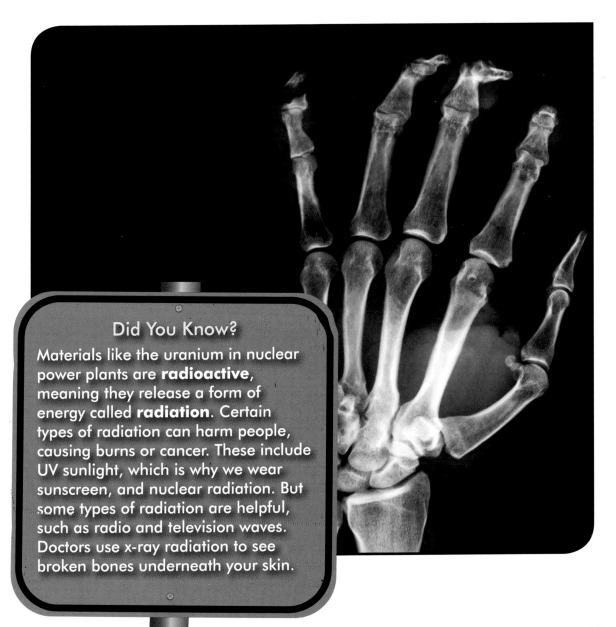

Did You Know?

Materials like the uranium in nuclear power plants are **radioactive**, meaning they release a form of energy called **radiation**. Certain types of radiation can harm people, causing burns or cancer. These include UV sunlight, which is why we wear sunscreen, and nuclear radiation. But some types of radiation are helpful, such as radio and television waves. Doctors use x-ray radiation to see broken bones underneath your skin.

In nuclear reactors, fission takes place in the core. Fuel rods containing the element uranium power the reactions. The reaction creates tremendous amounts of heat, so pipes constantly circulate cool water through the core to carry the heat away. In a nuclear reactor, water gets so hot it turns to steam. The steam turns a **turbine**, like a fan, which creates electricity to power homes and businesses.

Boiling Water Reactors

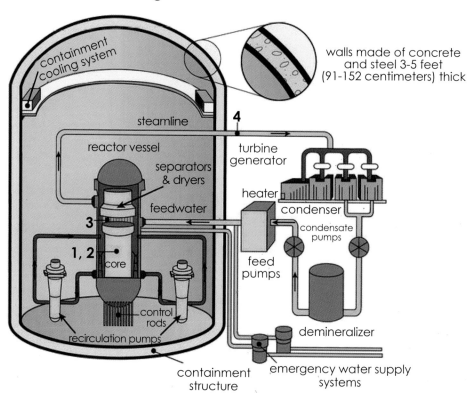

Boiling water reactors are one kind of nuclear reactor.
1. The nuclear reaction in the core creates heat.
2. That tremendous heat boils the water, creating steam.
3. Pipes carry the steam from the core to a turbine generator.
4. The steam turns the turbine generator, which creates the electricity.

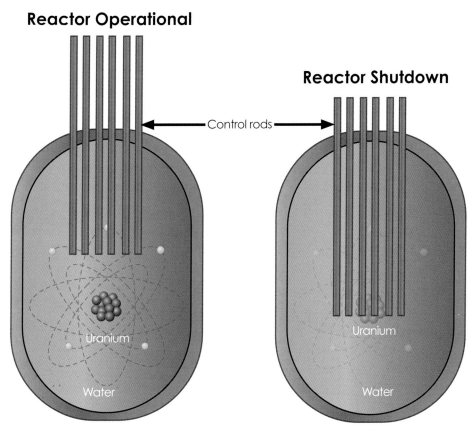

Reactor Operational

Reactor Shutdown

Control rods

Uranium

Uranium

Water

Water

If a reaction starts to get out of control, control rods plunge into the core automatically. These rods can be made of cadmium, boron, or other materials.

Control rods, also located in the core, can put the brakes on a nuclear reaction in case of emergency. Control rods are made of substances that absorb neutrons. Without neutrons to split atoms, the nuclear chain reaction stops. As an extra protective measure, the entire reactor is housed in a containment structure. It works like a protective shell, keeping radioactive material inside.

Nature's Nuclear Reactors

Nuclear reactors are not just manmade devices. Scientists discovered 14 natural reactors in uranium mines in what is now Gabon, Africa. They think the nuclear reactions have run off and on for almost 2 billion years.

Enrico Fermi
(1901–1954)

Enrico Fermi was originally from Italy, but he left the country when dictator Benito Mussolini came to power. Fermi won the Nobel Prize in 1938 for his work with radioactive elements and nuclear reactions.

In the US, the earliest experiments with nuclear energy began during World War II. On December 2, 1942, a team led by Enrico Fermi started the first controlled nuclear reaction. Enrico picked an unusual site for his reactor: a squash court under the abandoned football stands at the University of Chicago. Enrico's success paved the way for the development of nuclear bombs used during World War II.

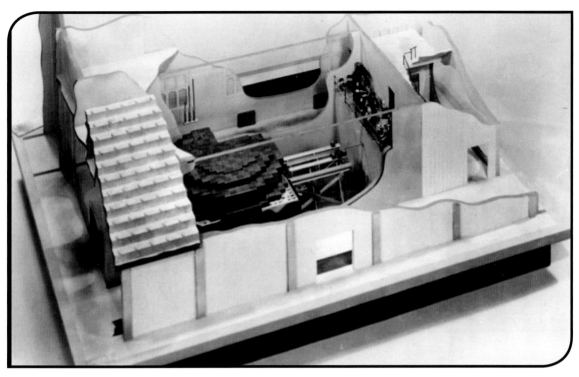

The first manmade nuclear reactors demonstrated the potential power of nuclear reactions. They paved the way for the nuclear bombs dropped on Japan during World War II.

Soon after the war ended, people began to harness nuclear power to create electricity. In 1948, Logan Emlet used a nuclear reactor in Oak Ridge, Tennessee to power a toy steam engine. It was the first time nuclear fission was used to generate electricity. By the 1950s, the first reactors were connected to power grids to bring electricity to homes and businesses.

On Sept. 3, 1948, Logan Emlet proved that a nuclear reactor could generate electricity. The Oak Ridge nuclear reactor, where Logan worked, was built in just 11 months and began operations in 1943.

Today, nuclear power is all around us. Ninety-nine nuclear power plants in the US create about 20 percent of the nation's electricity. In countries such as France, the number is much higher. About 75 percent of electricity there comes from nuclear power plants.

These cooling towers at a nuclear power plant release steam into the air after it is used to create electricity. The steam is not radioactive.

Still, nuclear energy does more than power homes and businesses. The US Navy uses nuclear energy to power 86 submarines and aircraft carriers. The National Aeronautics and Space Administration (NASA) relies on nuclear energy to power spacecraft like the New Horizons probe studying dwarf planet Pluto. NASA's Curiosity Mars rover uses nuclear power to drive around the Red Planet searching for water and the building blocks of life.

The Curiosity Mars Rover took this self portrait January 2015 near Mars's Mount Sharp. The Rover uses the camera at the end of its robotic arm to create these "selfies." It is the first of the Mars rovers to operate using nuclear power. Other rovers used solar energy.

Disaster Ahead

Nuclear meltdowns don't happen often, but when they do, their effects can circle the globe. When the Chernobyl reactor in modern-day Ukraine melted down, radioactive clouds swept through much of Europe. The Fukushima disaster dumped radioactive material into the Pacific Ocean.

Fast Fact
Small amounts of radioactive material turned up in blue fin tuna off the California coast after the Ukraine meltdown.

Ukrainian children were issued gas masks at school in case of a nuclear attack. This school, as well as the entire town of Pripyat, was abandoned after the nuclear disaster at Chernobyl.

Because meltdowns have worldwide effects, nuclear power plants are designed with backup systems to prevent accidents. During any type of emergency, the reactor immediately ends the chain reaction by plunging control rods into the core. But cooling the core to a safe level can take up to a month. This means cooling water must continue to circulate through the core carrying heat away. Two major problems can prevent this from happening: power outages and coolant leaks.

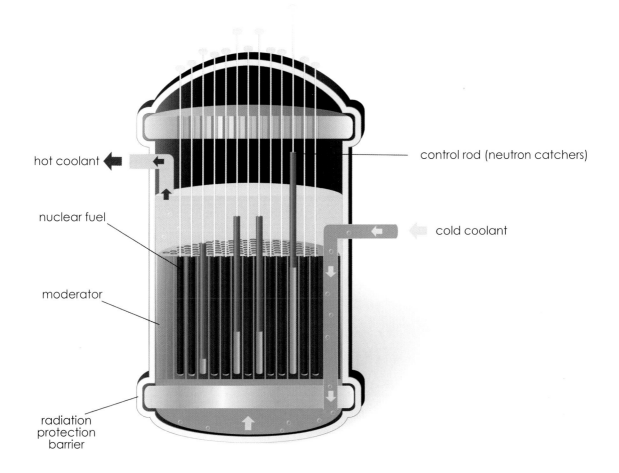

hot coolant

control rod (neutron catchers)

nuclear fuel

cold coolant

moderator

radiation protection barrier

Nuclear power plants normally use water as a coolant. This water may be pumped from a nearby river or even the sea. If a plant is not near a river or the ocean, the power plant may cool down the water and recirculate it through the core.

Electricity powers pumps that circulate cooling water through the core. Without electricity, pumps stop working and the core stays dangerously hot. To prevent meltdowns when the power goes out, nuclear power plants have backup generators. These generators are the size of large trucks and run on diesel fuel. If these fail, power plants have steam-powered systems that can run for several hours to cycle water through the core.

California's San Onofre Nuclear Generating Station was shut down because of problems with the steam-powered generators shown here. Radioactive water leaked out of one generator in January 2012. As of 2015, the plant remains closed.

After the September 11, 2001, terrorist attacks, the US Nuclear Regulatory Commission made sure plants were prepared for large fires or explosions from any source. Having backup generators ensures plants stay safe.

In the US, each power plant has a month's supply of diesel fuel as well as several portable generators and pumps if all other systems fail. Depots in Memphis, Tennessee, and Phoenix, Arizona, store replacement parts and spares that can be trucked to plants having emergencies.

Coolant leaks can also trigger meltdowns. If pipes carrying cool water to the core crack or break, the water escapes. Without enough water, temperatures in the core increase. Normally, the reactor senses water levels getting low and shuts down the nuclear reactions. Reactors also have backup systems to cool the core in the event of an emergency. These backup systems pull water from large storage tanks. Any water leaking from the system collects in a depression under the reactor. The emergency cooling system can recirculate that water through the core if needed.

The loss of coolant caused the nuclear disaster at Three Mile Island in Pennsylvania. An open valve allowed the coolant to bubble off and the nuclear core to melt down. It was the worst nuclear disaster in US history.

As a last line of defense, a containment building surrounds the reactor and all of its emergency systems. The building is designed to keep radioactive material inside in case of emergency. Containment buildings typically have concrete walls four feet (1.2 meters) thick. The walls are lined with steel and reinforced with steel bars.

Containment buildings serve as a last line of defense in a nuclear disaster. This French reactor uses a can-shaped building. Others look more like domes.

Nuclear power plants have several layers of protection. A structure called a reactor vessel acts as a containment structure around the core.

Containment buildings also protect nuclear power plants from possible outside dangers. They are designed to withstand natural disasters such as hurricanes, earthquakes, and tornadoes. They can hold up even if planes crash into them or explosions occur. These buildings protect against dangers both inside and out. Yet despite these safety measures, accidents sometimes happen.

Disasters in History

On March 28, 1979, the greatest nuclear disaster in the US unfolded at the Three Mile Island Nuclear Generating Station in Pennsylvania. A valve stuck in the open position allowed cooling water from one reactor to escape. More than 32,000 gallons (121,000 liters) of water—enough to fill two swimming pools—bubbled off. The reactor shut down as it should, but there was confusion in the control room. Faulty sensors meant operators couldn't tell what the problem was. The workers thought the cooling system had plenty of water, so they shut down the emergency cooling system. That system kept coolant flowing to the core. It was hours before workers turned the system back on. In the meantime, half the core melted.

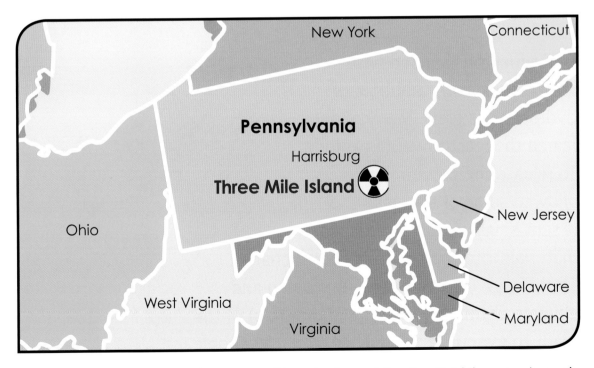

The Three Mile Island Nuclear Power Plant is about 10 miles (16 kilometers) south of Harrisburg, Pennsylvania, the state's capital city.

When planning for emergencies, nuclear power plant workers coordinate with people in local communities, as well as government officials.

As fuel rods reacted with water in the core, a bubble of hydrogen gas grew. Many people feared the reactor would explode. To release the pressure, workers allowed some of this gas to escape. It sent small amounts of radioactive materials into the sky. Governor Richard Thornburgh ordered pregnant women and children within five miles (8 kilometers) of the plant to **evacuate**. More than 140,000 people fled their homes in fear. Experts later said the amount of radiation released was almost harmless.

Three Mile Island (5 mile evacuation zone)

Eight years after Three Mile Island, the world's worst nuclear disaster occurred at the Chernobyl power plant near Pripyat, Ukraine. Nuclear workers performed a test of the reactor's backup systems at about 11 p.m. on April 25, 1986. Once the plant lost power, it typically took the plant's diesel backup generators 40 seconds to turn on. Workers wanted to know if the power plant could generate enough energy during those 40 seconds to power cooling pumps sending water through the core.

The Ukraine, site of the Chernobyl disaster, was part of the Soviet Union when the accident happened. Fifteen republics formed the Soviet Union, including Russia, Belarus, and Moldova.

For the test, workers slowed down the nuclear reactions by inserting control rods to absorb neutrons. But when the reactions slowed too much, workers began to remove the control rods. The reaction quickly spun out of control. When workers tried to reinsert the control rods, they bent and the reaction raged on.

What made it worse: the workers had shut down the backup cooling system for the test.

Yuri Korneev worked on the turbine at the Chernobyl plant. He remembers explosions and crumbling concrete raining down from the roof. A heavy piece of metal landed a few yards from him. He was lucky to survive.

The Chernobyl disaster rated a 7 on the scale commonly used to judge nuclear accidents. It was one of the worst nuclear accidents to date.

When workers couldn't get the core to cool fast enough, two explosions ripped through the containment structure. Unlike most other nations, the then-Soviet Union used weaker, concrete-only structures. Large amounts of radiation filled the air. Thirty workers died that day or within weeks. More than 6,000 young people developed cancer as a result of radiation exposure.

Chernobyl (19 mile evacuation zone)

On the 25th anniversary of the Chernobyl disaster, the Ukraine unveiled a new memorial to recognize the victims and heroes of the accident. The memorial is in the capital city of Kiev.

The earthquake that struck Fukushima, Japan on March 11, 2011, damaged buildings and cut power to the Daiichi nuclear power plant. Three of the six reactors were down for maintenance when the earthquake happened. At the three remaining reactors, control rods stopped the nuclear reactions as planned, and diesel backups started to make electricity. Then the second tsunami wave, four stories tall, flooded the generators.

The Tohoku Earthquake was the fourth largest to strike Japan. The earthquake and resulting tsunami devastated northeast Japan. People hundreds of miles away felt the quake.

The Fukushima Daiichi Power Station was one of 17 power plants in Japan at the time of the disaster. Together they produced about 30 percent of the nation's electricity.

The situation was especially bad at reactor number one, where melting fuel rods mixed with steam. A cloud of explosive hydrogen gas built up. A team of six workers took turns bravely entering the heart of the reactor to open a vent, allowing the explosive gas and radioactive material to escape. The reactor exploded anyway. Explosions also rocked the other two reactors.

During a cleanup operation following the Fukushima Daiichi nuclear meltdown, workers dump radiation-contaminated leaves and soil into bags for disposal.

Ultimately, Japanese emergency workers used fire trucks and helicopters to douse the fire and keep cool water flowing to the cores. But the process took weeks. In the meantime, the evacuation zone spread to 20 miles (32 kilometers) around the plant and included 80,000 people. Many people are still waiting for the cleanup to end so they can return to their homes.

Fukushima Daiichi (20 mile evacuation zone)

Dealing with Disasters

Nuclear meltdowns are unique disaster situations. In many emergencies, police officers and firefighters form the first line of defense. But during a meltdown, nuclear plant workers are the first responders. Twenty-four hours a day, power plant operators and technicians working in the control rooms monitor the plant's health, like a pilot watches cockpit displays. When something goes wrong, workers are the first to see the alarms. Although shutdowns happen automatically in an emergency, workers can manually shut down the reaction and start emergency cooling.

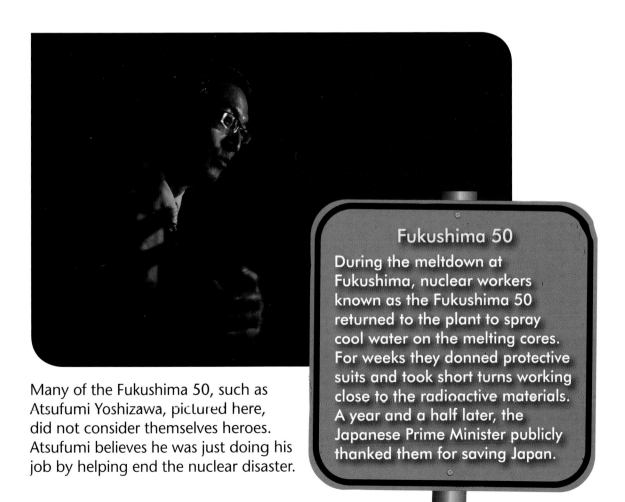

Many of the Fukushima 50, such as Atsufumi Yoshizawa, pictured here, did not consider themselves heroes. Atsufumi believes he was just doing his job by helping end the nuclear disaster.

Fukushima 50

During the meltdown at Fukushima, nuclear workers known as the Fukushima 50 returned to the plant to spray cool water on the melting cores. For weeks they donned protective suits and took short turns working close to the radioactive materials. A year and a half later, the Japanese Prime Minister publicly thanked them for saving Japan.

Workers wear personal protective suits to shield themselves during a meltdown. This includes jumpsuits, facemasks, hard hats, gloves, and boots to protect against hazardous chemicals. However, no suit protects workers against harmful radiation. Like medical x-rays, radiation easily penetrates clothes, skin, and organs. Therefore, part of workers' gear includes radiation dosimeters to measure how much radiation workers receive over time. Only limiting time spent near radiation or staying farther away from the source can protect workers when they respond to a meltdown.

Protective suits ensure workers don't touch dangerous chemicals in the plant. Workers wear face masks or respirators so they don't breathe in poisonous chemicals.

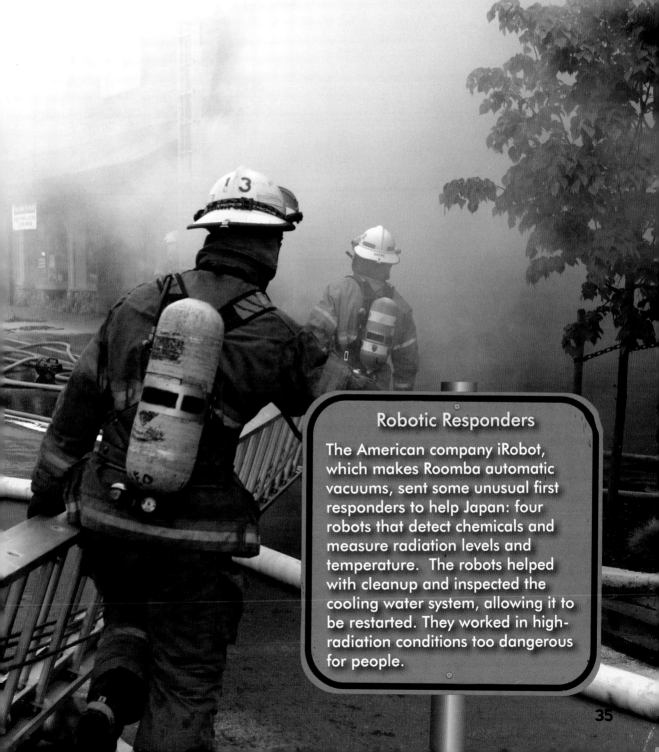

If nuclear workers can't prevent a meltdown, police and firemen provide backup. Nuclear plants often have their own firefighters and security forces. If needed, the plant may call on local police and fire stations to help.

Robotic Responders

The American company iRobot, which makes Roomba automatic vacuums, sent some unusual first responders to help Japan: four robots that detect chemicals and measure radiation levels and temperature. The robots helped with cleanup and inspected the cooling water system, allowing it to be restarted. They worked in high-radiation conditions too dangerous for people.

International Nuclear Event Scale

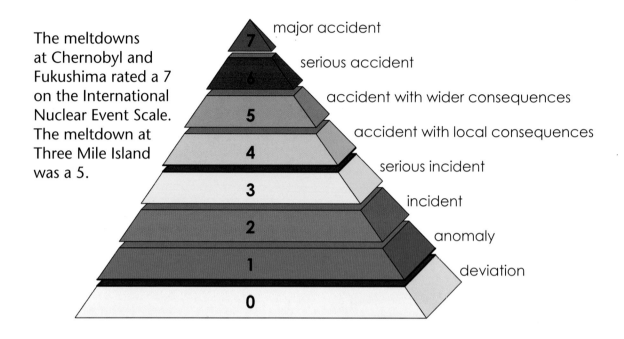

The meltdowns at Chernobyl and Fukushima rated a 7 on the International Nuclear Event Scale. The meltdown at Three Mile Island was a 5.

7 — major accident
6 — serious accident
5 — accident with wider consequences
4 — accident with local consequences
3 — serious incident
2 — incident
1 — anomaly
0 — deviation

During the Chernobyl and Fukushima disasters, military pilots and firefighters responded. At Fukushima, military pilots flew helicopters with special shielding 300 feet (91 meters) above the power plant, dumping water to keep a fuel storage pool filled. Military pilots during Chernobyl dumped sand from 80 aircraft to stop the meltdown.

The Japanese military used Chinook helicopters to scoop up sea water and dump it on the Fukushima Daiichi plant.

Firefighters at Fukushima pumped seawater into the reactors and storage pools. When a meltdown happens, it's all hands on deck!

The US has systems in place to warn people about nuclear emergencies. People who live within ten miles (16 kilometers) of nuclear power plants receive instructions annually on how to respond to nuclear incidents.

Depending on what happens, sirens within the ten mile (16 kilometer) zone might go off. These tell people to listen to the radio or TV for instructions. People may be asked to evacuate or stay inside a house, school, or other building.

The nationwide Emergency Alert System in the US uses television and radio to let people know about emergencies, including nuclear meltdowns. Cell phones can receive emergency alerts too.

During a nuclear emergency people should follow a few simple steps. If evacuating, keep car windows rolled up and turn off vents to keep outside air from entering the car. When seeking shelter in a building, interior rooms without windows and basements provide the best protection. Also turn off heaters, air conditioning, and vents that pull in air from outside.

After the Chernobyl accident, the Soviet government declared a large area uninhabitable forever and relocated thousands of people from their homes. About a thousand people ignored the government and returned to the area. About 200 people, mostly women, still live there. They have electricity but no running water and must grow their own food.

People should keep emergency kits in their cars in case they have to evacuate. Kits should include extra medications, extra clothes and bedding, and copies of important documents such as drivers' licenses and birth certificates.

In Japan, workers dig up several inches of topsoil, which is contaminated with radiation. The soil is hauled from the area. The cleanup has cost more than $13 billion.

Cleaning up after a nuclear meltdown can take years because radioactive materials take decades to break down and become safe. Liko Kanno evacuated her vegetable farm shortly after the Fukushima disaster. Radiation contaminated the soil, and she could no longer farm there. More than three years later, she still lives in a temporary house outside Fukushima. More than 500 workers worked to decontaminate her village. They dug out topsoil filled with radiation and wiped down buildings. Residents wonder if they will ever be able to return.

Fast Fact

Exposure to high levels of radiation can cause nausea, vomiting, diarrhea, headache, fever, and death. People exposed to high levels of radiation also are more likely to get thyroid cancer or leukemia.

In the Ukraine, the government declared all land within 18 miles (29 kilometers) of the Chernobyl plant uninhabitable. The area remained a ghost town. Nearby Pripyat, also abandoned, has become a wildlife preserve. It is home to falcons, bears, wolves, endangered bison, and wild horses. Despite lingering radiation, some people are moving back to the area, and tourists are traveling to the region.

Each year the International Red Cross and Red Crescent societies monitor 90,000 people from the Chernobyl area for signs of thyroid cancer. It's the society's longest-running humanitarian program.

Keeping Citizens Safe

In the US, the Nuclear Regulatory Commission (NRC) oversees all nuclear power plants. Whenever nuclear accidents happen, the NRC reviews its rules. For example, a big part of the problem at Three Mile Island was confusion and lack of training. As a result of the disaster, nuclear workers now train on simulators, much like pilots train on flight simulators.

Following the disaster at Fukushima, the NRC took several actions. This included reviewing all US plants to make sure they could withstand the risks of earthquakes or flooding at their sites. US plants also made plans to operate without power for long periods of time.

The head of the NRC visited the Fukushima Daiichi emergency response center after the disaster. After studying the event closely, the NRC developed 12 recommendations that US nuclear power plants must implement.

Floating reactors developed at the Massachusetts Institute of Technology would be built on land. Once complete, boats would tow the reactors out to be attached to the sea floor.

Scientists and engineers continue to explore options for making nuclear power safer. Scientists from the Massachusetts Institute of Technology (MIT) have proposed building nuclear power plants offshore on floating platforms. Locating the core below the ocean's surface would eliminate the need for electric pumps to circulate the cool ocean water. Floating reactors would also be safe from earthquakes and tsunamis. Tsunami waves are small offshore, growing several stories high as they near the coast.

> **Fast Fact**
>
> Some scientists are developing bacteria that munch on nuclear waste. These bacteria create a hard shell around uranium, so it can't leak into soil or groundwater.

Countries such as India and China are experimenting with thorium rather than uranium as fuel for power plants. Thorium is three times more abundant than uranium. Because it's plentiful, it's also cheaper. Used thorium loses its radioactivity far faster than uranium. There are also less radioactive leftovers, because thorium is more efficient.

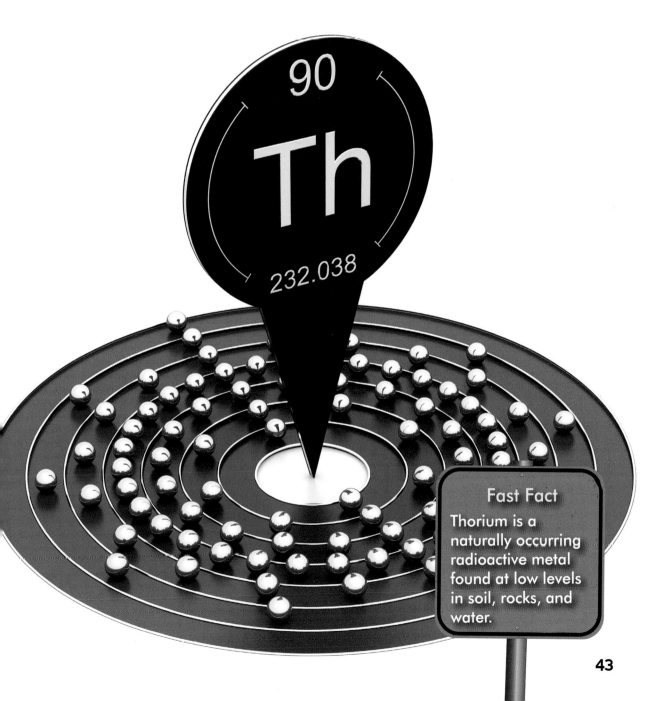

90

Th

232.038

Fast Fact

Thorium is a naturally occurring radioactive metal found at low levels in soil, rocks, and water.

Nuclear power remains a hot-button issue. Some argue that we will have to rely more on nuclear power to reduce our use of fossil fuels such as coal and oil. Others argue that the risks of meltdowns and radiation sickness are too great. For now, nuclear power is here to stay. And scientists are working to make it safer.

How You Can Help When Disaster Strikes

- Review www.ready.gov to learn what to do immediately following a nuclear disaster.
- Collect clothing, toys, and hygiene items such as shampoo, soap, and toothbrushes for people living in temporary shelters.
- Organize a fundraiser to help victims. Try a lemonade stand, bake sale, or walkathon. Donate the money to aid organizations such as the International Federation of Red Cross and Red Crescent Societies (ifrc.org).
- Write thank you notes to military personnel, firefighters, and police officers involved in disaster cleanup.

Glossary

atoms (AT-uhmz): smallest parts of a substance that can't be divided

cores (KORZ): parts of a nuclear reactor where the reaction takes place

electrons (i-LEK-trahnz): small, negatively charged particles that orbit the atom's nucleus

evacuate (i-VAK-yoo-ate): to leave because a place is dangerous

generators (JEN-uh-ray-turz): machines that make electricity

meltdown (MELT-doun): when a nuclear reactor's core melts releasing radiation

neutrons (NOO-trahnz): small particles with no charge contained in an atom's nucleus

nuclear energy (NOO-klee-ur EN-ur-jee): energy created by splitting apart atoms

nucleus (NOO-klee-uhs): center of an atom made up of neutrons and protons

protons (PROH-tahnz): small, positively charged particles contained in an atom's nucleus

radiation (ray-dee-AY-shuhn): particles given off by the nuclei of radioactive substances

radioactive (ray-dee-oh-ak-tiv): giving off particles released by nuclear energy

tsunami (tsu-NAH-mee): large wave caused by an undersea earthquake or volcano

turbine (tuhr-BINE): a device that spins to create power

uranium (yu-RAY-nee-uhm): radioactive chemical element used to create nuclear energy

Index

Show What You Know

1. How is nuclear energy created?
2. What are some problems that lead to nuclear meltdowns?
3. Which nuclear disaster was worse, Chernobyl or Fukushima? Why?
4. What are some ways to stay safe during a nuclear emergency?
5. How would you feel about living near a nuclear power plant? Give reasons to explain your answer.

Websites to Visit

www.eia.gov/kids/energy.cfm?page=nuclear_home-basics

www.nrc.gov/reading-rm/basic-ref/students.html

www.pbs.org/wgbh/amex/three

About the Author

Kirsten W. Larson spent six years at NASA before writing for young people. She's written books and magazine articles about everything from space potties to animal vampires and mammoth bones, all in the name of science. She lives with her husband and two children near Los Angeles, California.

The author would like to thank Scott Burnell at the Nuclear Regulatory Commission for his assistance with this book.

Meet The Author!
www.meetREMauthors.com

www.rourkeeducationalmedia.com

PHOTO CREDITS: Cover © Pool/Corbis; Title Page © MichaelUtech ; page 4 © Yoshiyuki Kaneko; page 5, 27 © pavalena; page 6 © Digital Globe / Science Source; page 7, 12, 20, 24, 26, 41 © NRC; page 8 © mTaira; page 9 © Allied Navy/Wikipedia; page 11 © Stockdevil; page 13 © Jen Thomas; page 14 © Department of Energy/Wikipedia; page 15 © Argonne National Laboratory, Oak Ridge National Laboratory; page 16 © RelaxFoto.de; page 17 © NASA/PL-Caltech/MSSS; page 18, 38 © alexkuehni; page 19 © Designua; page 21 © arnet117; page 22 © Dobresum; page 25 © halepak; page 28 © toonmeuris; page 29 © www.kremlin.ru; page 30 © Yoshiyayo; page 31 © HO/Reuters/Corbis; page 32 © Greg Baker/AP/Corbis; page 33, 39 © ISSEI KATO/Reuters/Corbis; page 34 © Ivan Bliznetsov; page 35 © renal; page 36 © Silverspoon, YOMIURI/Reuters/Corbis; page 37 © scyther5; page 40 © SERDAR YAGCI; page 42 © InSapphoWeTrust; page 43 © Concept W; page 44 © CUNEYT HIZAL; page 45 © Jason Verschoor

Edited by: Keli Sipperley
Cover and interior design by: Jen Thomas

Library of Congress PCN Data

Nuclear Meltdowns/Kirsten W. Larson
(Devastating Disasters)
ISBN 978-1-63430-428-3 (hard cover)
ISBN 978-1-63430-528-0 (soft cover)
ISBN 978-1-63430-618-8 (e-Book)
Library of Congress Control Number: 2015931851

Printed in the United States of America, North Mankato, Minnesota

Also Available as:
ROURKE'S
e-Books